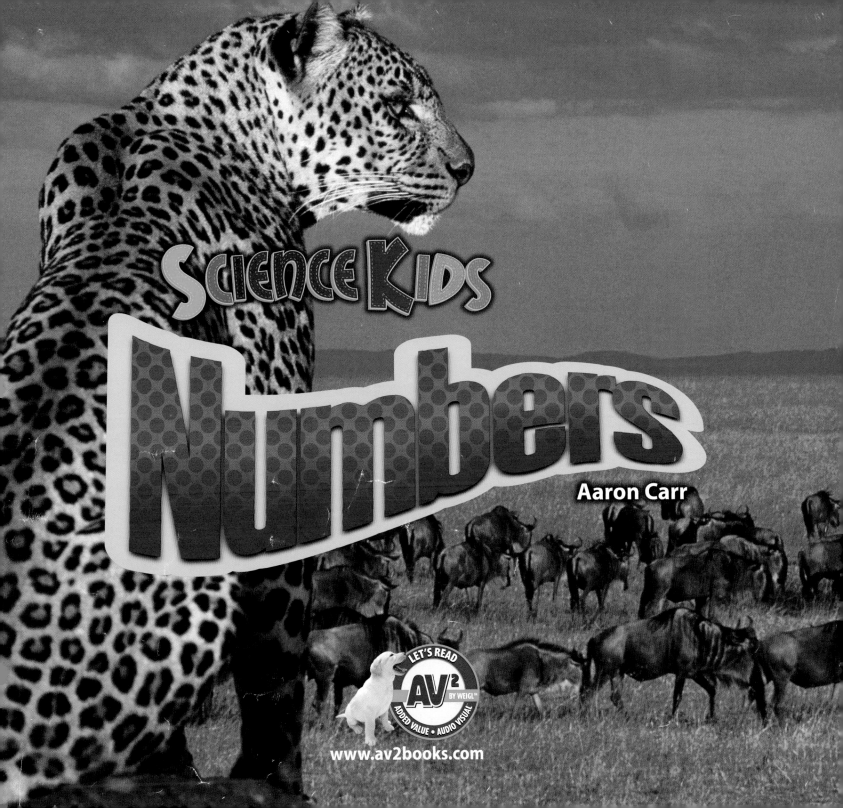

SCIENCE KIDS

Numbers

Aaron Carr

AV²
BY WEIGL™
LET'S READ · ADDED VALUE · AUDIO VISUAL

Go to **www.av2books.com**, and enter this book's unique code.

BOOK CODE

Q 3 5 9 7

AV² by Weigl brings you media enhanced books that support active learning.

AV² provides enriched content that supplements and complements this book. Weigl's AV² books strive to create inspired learning and engage young minds in a total learning experience.

Your AV² Media Enhanced books come alive with...

Audio
Listen to sections of the book read aloud.

Video
Watch informative video clips.

Embedded Weblinks
Gain additional information for research.

Try This!
Complete activities and hands-on experiments.

Key Words
Study vocabulary, and complete a matching word activity.

Quizzes
Test your knowledge.

Slide Show
View images and captions, and prepare a presentation.

... and much, much more!

Published by AV² by Weigl
350 5th Avenue, 59th Floor New York, NY 10118
Website: www.av2books.com www.weigl.com

Library of Congress Control Number: 2012941986
ISBN 978-1-61913-086-9 (hardcover)
ISBN 978-1-61913-756-1 (softcover)

Printed in the United States of America in North Mankato, Minnesota
1 2 3 4 5 6 7 8 9 16 15 14 13 12

062012
WEP170512

Project Coordinator: Aaron Carr   Design: Mandy Christiansen

Weigl acknowledges Getty Images, iStock, and Dreamstime as image suppliers for this title.

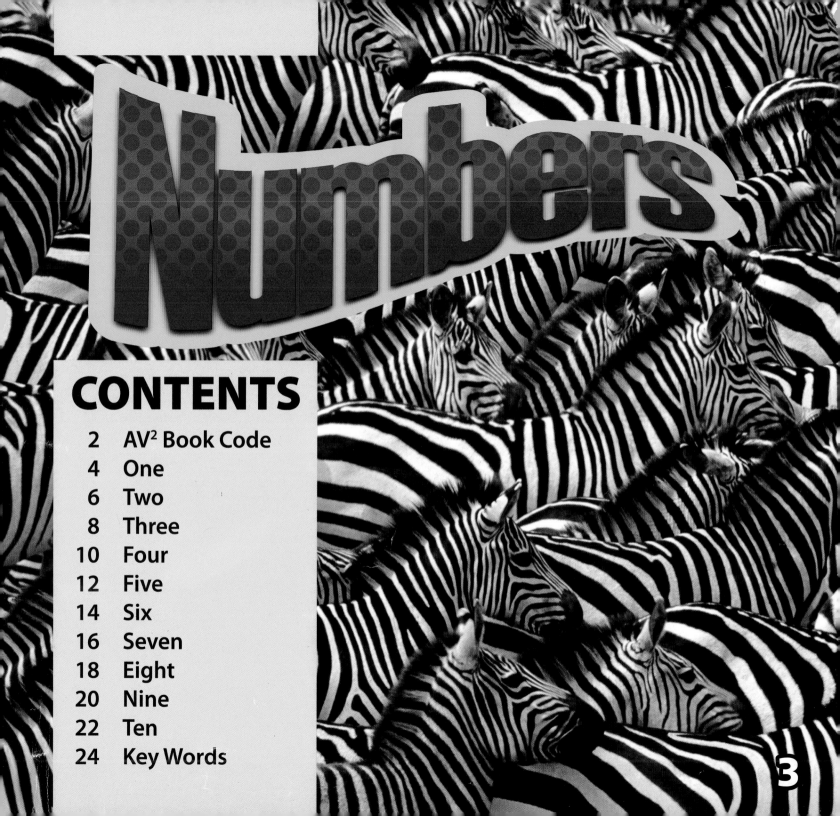

Numbers

CONTENTS

1

one

1

There is
one cheetah.

5

2

two

1 2

There are
two gazelles.

7

three

● ● ●
1 2 3

There are three zebras.

4

four

● ● ● ●

1 2 3 4

There are
four elephants.

5

five

● ● ● ● ●
1 2 3 4 5

There are
five gorillas.

13

six

● ● ● ● ● ●
1 2 3 4 5 6

There are
six meerkats.

7

seven

1 2 3 4 5 6 7

There are
seven flamingos.

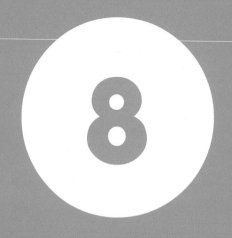

8

eight

1 2 3 4 5 6 7 8

There are
eight giraffes.

nine

1 2 3 4 5 6 7 8 9

There are nine lemurs.

10

ten

● ● ● ● ● ● ● ● ● ●
1 2 3 4 5 6 7 8 9 10

There are
ten lions.

KEY WORDS

Research has shown that as much as 65 percent of all written material published in English is made up of 300 words. These 300 words cannot be taught using pictures or learned by sounding them out. They must be recognized by sight. This book contains 7 common sight words to help young readers improve their reading fluency and comprehension. This book also teaches young readers several important content words, such as proper nouns. These words are paired with pictures to aid in learning and improve understanding.

Sight Words

are	there
four	three
is	two
one	

Content Words

cheetah	gorillas
elephants	lemurs
flamingos	lions
gazelles	meerkats
giraffes	zebras

Check out www.av2books.com for activities, videos, audio clips, and more!

1 Go to www.av2books.com.

2 Enter book code.

Q 3 5 9 7

3 Fuel your imagination online!

www.av2books.com